Welcome to LIFESEARCH!

If you urgently need to prepare to lead a LIFESEARCH group, turn the page and read QUICKLEAD. QUICKLEAD will give you enough information to get started.

L IFESEARCH hopes to help you and other persons within a small group explore topics about which you are concerned in your everyday living. We've tried to make LIFESEARCH

✔ immediately helpful to you;

✔ filled with practical ideas;

✔ Christian-oriented and biblically based;

✔ group building, so you will find companions in your mutual struggles and learning;

✔ easy for anyone to lead.

You have probably chosen to join with others in studying this LIFE-SEARCH book because you feel some need. You may feel that need in your life strongly. Our hope for you is that by the time you complete the six chapters in this book with your LIFESEARCH group, you will have

✔ a better handle on how to meet the need you feel;

✔ some greater insights into yourself;

✔ a deeper understanding of how Christian faith can help you meet that need;

✔ a more profound relationship with God;

✔ new and/or richer relationships with the other persons in your LIFESEARCH group.

If you discover nothing else as part of this LIFESEARCH experience, we want you to learn this fact: *that you are not alone as you face life*. Other people have faced and still face the same problems, struggles, demands, and needs that you face. Some have advice to offer. Some have learned things the hard way— things they can now tell you about. Some can help you think through and talk through old concerns and new insights. Some can listen as you share what you've tried and what you want to achieve. Some even need what you can offer.

And you will never be alone because God stands with you.

The secret to LifeSearch is in the workings of your group. No two LifeSearch groups will ever be alike. Your LifeSearch group is made up of unique individuals—including you. All of you have much to offer one another. This Life-Search book simply provides a framework for you and your group to work together in learning about an area of mutual concern.

We would like to hear what you think about LifeSearch and ways you can suggest for improving future LifeSearch books. A Mail-In Feedback survey appears in the back. Whether you lead the group or participate in it, please take the time to fill out the survey and mail it in to us.

IF YOU ARE LEADING A Life-Search GROUP, please read the articles in the back of this book. These LifeSearch group leadership articles may answer the questions you have about leading your group.

IF YOU ARE PARTICIPATING IN A LifeSearch GROUP, BUT NOT LEADING IT, please read at least the article, "If You're Not Leading the Group." In any case, **you will benefit most if you come to your group meeting having read the chapter ahead of time and having attempted any assignments given in the previous chapter's "Before Next Time" sections.**

We want to remain helpful to you throughout your LifeSearch group experience. If you have any questions about using this LifeSearch book, please feel free to call Curric-U-Phone at 1-800-251-8591, and ask for the LifeSearch editor.

QUICKLEAD™

Look here for **QUICK** information about how to **LEAD** a session of LIFE-SEARCH. On LIFESEARCH pages, look for the following:

ICONS
Seven kinds of icons suggest different kinds of activities for your group to do at different points during the session (see page 4 for more information about ICONS).

MAIN TEXT: the "meat" of the session. Hopefully everyone will have read the MAIN TEXT ahead of time; if not, be prepared to offer a brief summary of the MAIN TEXT in your own words.

MARGINAL NOTES give you activity instructions and additional discussion starters.

CHAPTER THREE

LOOK BEYOND: WHAT DOES THE WORLD NEED NOW?

WORSHIP

Begin by praying this prayer:

O God of all people and places, we thank you for the marvelous diversity that you have created and placed in this world. We praise you for loving the world so much that you sent your son to be the light of this world. Inspire us to allow your loving light to shine in us and through us that the world might be transformed. In Christ's name, Amen.

CHECKING IN

Begin this session by welcoming any new persons to the group. Invite anyone to share significant events that may have occurred in their life since last time.

This time you will be looking beyond yourselves and the needs of persons in your congregation to the needs of persons in the world. Last time you were encouraged to visit a homeless shelter or community food pantry in your community or area. Or you may have visited a jail or talked with someone who works with the poor. These visits were intended to open your eyes to the needs of people in your area as you begin to reflect on how God wants to use your gifts for the transformation of the world into a community of justice and love.

DISCUSSION POINT

Debrief the members of the group on their visits using these questions and/or other questions as appropriate.

Spend some time reflecting on your visit to a shelter or food pantry. How many people does the shelter or pantry serve each month? Where do they get their resources? Where do they get their volunteers? Did you meet any of the clients of the shelter or pantry? How did you feel about being in such a setting? Does anyone in your group volunteer in ministries to the poor? What assistance does your church provide to the agencies that serve the poor? Has your church considered providing food or lodging for the poor? How does your congregation respond to emergency needs in your community? Who ministers to the needs of persons in jail or prison in your community? Has anyone in your congregation or community been on a short-term work-camp in this country or abroad? Has your community or area experienced a natural disaster such as a flood, earthquake, or hurricane? How did the church respond in that crisis? Are there any missionaries in your congregation or community who might reflect with you on the broader needs of our world? Please use these questions as a way to focus your attention on the needs of people beyond your own congregation.

If the group identifies such a missionary and wishes to do so, invite him or her to an extra session of your group to help members reflect about the needs around them.

SPIRITUAL GIFTS

UNDERLINED TEXT identify discussion starters inside the MAIN TEXT.

For more information, read the **LEADERSHIP ARTICLES** in the back of this LIFESEARCH book.

ICONS

ICONS are picture/symbols that show you at a glance what you should do with different parts of the main text at different times in the LIFESEARCH sessions.

The seven kinds of icons are

 WORSHIP—A prayer, hymn, or other act of worship is suggested at this place in the MAIN TEXT.

 CHECKING IN—At the beginning of each session, LIFESEARCH group members will be asked to "check in" with each other about what is happening in their lives. Sometimes group members will also be asked to "check in" about how their LIFESEARCH group experience seems to them.

 DISCUSSION POINT—Either the MAIN TEXT or a MARGINAL NOTE will suggest discussion starters. You will probably find more DISCUSSION POINTS than you can use in the usual LIFESEARCH session.

 GROUP INTERACTION—Either the MAIN TEXT or a MARGINAL NOTE will suggest a group activity that goes beyond a simple discussion within the whole group.

 BIBLE STUDY—At least once each session, your LIFESEARCH group will study a Bible passage together. Usually, DISCUSSION POINTS and/or GROUP INTERACTIONS are part of the BIBLE STUDY.

 WRITTEN REFLECTION—The MAIN TEXT will contain one or more suggestions for individuals to reflect personally on an issue. Space will be provided within the MAIN TEXT for writing down reflections. Sometimes individuals will be invited to share their written reflections if they wish.

 BEFORE NEXT TIME—In most sessions, your LIFESEARCH group members will be asked to do something on their own before the next time you meet together.

INTRODUCTION

"While we eat lunch, I'm going to interview you," I said.

"Oh, no! I hope it's not about stress!", he said.

It was.

Preparing to write this book, I interviewed persons from their mid twenties to late sixties. You will find many statements throughout this book that originated in these interviews. I am grateful to those I interviewed, for people generously went inside themselves to search for answers to my questions. They returned with gifts of tears and laughter, humor and pain, longing and certainty, and a certain amount of *stress*.

My preference would be to gather us all together, them and you, in the midst of all the helpful, warm, serious, technical, rational, and irrational books that fell into my hands off bookshelves. If we could talk face to face and read gems of wisdom to each other, if we could talk about how we experience stress, saying what we think about it all, we would surely then go out and change the world. We would make it a better place, a less stressful place, to live for all people.

Since we can't change the world, how shall we get a handle on our lives? What will it take for us to personally accept all the valid help around us—in Scripture, through persons, and elsewhere, and learn to live our stressed lives as Christians?

I have resisted writing down for you the treasured words from books, magazines, and even cartoons that illuminate the subject of stress. Many helps are based on scientific research, but are clearly readable for you and me. They yield important information to help ground our understanding of the role of stress in our lives: this is what stress is; this is how it acts; this is what will happen if we do not manage our responses to it.

Some words are richly quotable. I simply determined not to use them because there are so many. If you want to go further after this LIFESEARCH study, I strongly recommend a trip to the library or a bookstore. You will be stimulated, fed, and inspired to improve your handling of stress. If you cannot read but one medical-type book, read *Type A Behavior and Your Heart*, by Friedman and Roseman (Ballantine Books, 1974). Although written about heart attacks, it is a helpful stress management book. It packs in a great deal of information about you and me, described as either Type A or Type B personalities, and our reactions to life. Unlike many of the other good books, it's often available at discount and grocery stores!

> *"If it is difficult to define and measure stress, it is even more difficult to calculate its cost. It costs an inordinate amount in terms of human misery. Eight out of every ten persons surveyed in a recent national poll said that they need less stress in their lives. Several hundred studies have shown a relationship between stress, such as divorce or change in career, and development of disease. In addition to absenteeism, stress leads to poor industrial relations, poor productivity, conflicts, official and unofficial strikes, high staff turnover, job dissatisfaction, and industrial accidents.*
>
> (From *The Complete Guide to Stress Management*, by Chandra Patel; Plenum Press, 1991, page 4.)

Many of the most learned physician/writers either lack religious education or the courage to reveal all they know about stress for fear of being judged nonscientific. I wanted them to talk not only about the body and the mind, but the spirit. Blessedly, some of them do. They are the ones, along with our gifted spiritual authors, who offer the deepest, most balanced help.

I like one author who scorns all the credit stress gets for affecting us. He declares again and again that it is not stress that kills us, but the way we react to it.

One of the main facts I have learned about stress from reading, watching TV and films (by both experts and "lay consumers of stress"), doing interviews, and living my own life is that no matter how much a person knows, we are all vulnerable people.

The mightiest among us, in every field, have fallen because of inability to handle stress. What are we going to do about this life condition that isn't going away soon? We are not going back to great-grandma's time, which we fantasize as being slow and peaceful.

Stress today is a fact of life, both public and private. Can Christians be expected to respond to stress differently from anyone else? Can doing this study within our church community count? If not, it will just fill one more block of time when we could be doing something else, giving ourselves needed space to live the lives we want to lead.

The study can count only if we take it personally and let God use it in our lives. Let's risk it!

Mary Dell Miles has written for *Birmingham* magazine and for various business and church periodicals.

As a Christian educator, Ms. Miles has served on the staffs of workshops for adults and youth at every level of the church, including the general church. She has served as program coordinator for an annual United Methodist seminar for youth on national and international affairs and has traveled in the former Soviet Union and China with college young adult groups for the purpose of studying the cultures of these nations.

Ms. Miles has two grown children, Mike and Lynn. She resides in Birmingham, Alabama where she is professionally employed with a computer services corporation and is an active volunteer at First United Methodist Church. Ms. Miles is a graduate of Huntingdon College.

CHAPTER ONE

TIME OUT TO THINK ABOUT STRESS

We are paying an exorbitant price for living in our uptight, stress-filled world. We like to think we can live at our own hectic pace, abusing our bodies . . . and never missing a beat as we grab all the gusto we can . . . . Some hard driving executives have already accepted the fact that in the near future they will need a triple heart bypass. It seems . . . some kind of proof that they have given their all in the competitive drive for corporate success (From *The Art of Staying Well in an Uptight World*, by Ken Olson; Oliver Nelson, 1989; page 12).

She lost three sons and a daughter to sudden, tragic deaths, and one to mental illness. She never left the church but only seemed to draw nearer to it. Her Christian faith expressed itself in serenity, love, and strength, with gratitude for all her blessings. Her remaining family arose and called her blessed.

A young professional baseball player developed a tumor in his pitching arm. The tumor was cut out but it returned. Eventually, he had to give up the game he loved. He lived through incredible suffering, both physical and otherwise. Through great losses, different kinds of "wins" emerged, including a tremendous Christian witness. His life counted.

In a southern city a mother moved her son to a different neighborhood to find a safer place for him to grow up. He was well accepted and became a leader at church and at school. One night after a football game in which he had given tremendous leadership, his life was taken in a drive-by shooting by people who did not even know him. In the midst of community outrage and grief, his mother was a pillar of strength to others. At graduation, she accepted his diploma and said, "This means so much to me. I ask everyone who knew him to take a stand for what he stood for. Change."

A famous championship coach, fired once for losing, lived calmly within the stressful life of college athletics, a life he had chosen. Persons knew his philosophy well enough that they could say it for him: "Winning football games is a lot of fun, but there's a lot of pressure with it, too. People have forgotten it's just a game. Sometimes you learn more by losing. A lot of things are more important to me than winning a football game: Jesus Christ and my family for starters." Based on the time he had for each, including his adult son with mental retardation, people knew he meant what he said.

Responding to Life's Ups and Downs

On the Mount of Olives, Jesus' sweat became like great drops of blood (Luke 22:44) because he was under ultimate stress. In the great stories of our faith recorded throughout our Scriptures, Adam and Eve, their children Cain and Abel, Abraham and Sarah, and others faced moments, days, even years of stress.

DISCUSSION POINT

Is some stress essential for our very existence? for personal growth?

Does stress (in manageable doses, of course) release our human creativity?

The earliest members of the human race faced stress from hunger, the need for protection from the elements, relationships with those around them, illness, death, and other situations of great difficulty. Yet today, despite modern progress, we live with stress levels unknown before. With large populations, crowded conditions, the explosion of technology, competition, and contemporary thinking, we find ourselves in a world that seems unmanageable. Often life seems painful and hard. While not everyone feels stressed, too many of us do.

Dr. Ken Olson, in his book *The Art of Staying Well in an Uptight World* (Oliver Nelson, 1989) reminds us again of the fragile relationships of health and stress management:

DISCUSSION POINT

To what extent have you experienced the wear and tear of chronic stress described by Ken Olson?

"These days it is difficult to stay healthy in our uptight world. I believe that seventy to eighty percent of the people going to physicians are ill not because of an infectious disease caused by a germ, but because of the wear and tear of too much chronic stress in their lives. There is no pill to cure their sickness, no surgical procedure that will remove its root cause. If people are sick from an infectious germ or "mysterious virus," we know that traumatic and chronic stress disrupt and weaken the effectiveness of the immune system to destroy invaders" (page 11).

Most of us, even those of us who call ourselves Christians, are caught up and conditioned by our culture. With unreasonably high expectations, we have trouble with relationships. Told that material success will make us happy, too few of us love our work. Deciding that personal freedom is a number one priority, we lose our balance and wreck our lives. We are not even satisfied by our play. While many in the U.S.A. have more than we need, many live with fear that we will never be secure because it takes so much "stuff" to live in the world as we know it.

DISCUSSION POINT

On a scale from one to ten, with ten being the highest, at what level do you feel stress at this moment?

At what level do you usually feel stress every day?

At its worst, to what level does stress reach for you?

DISCUSSION POINT

CHECKING IN

At the top of a piece of newsprint or chalkboard write, "THIS IS OUR GROUP." Continue writing as members take turns calling out words. Discuss the accuracy of your group description. Revise the description if necessary to capture more fully and fairly who you are as a group. When this task is complete, say together, "This is who we are. God have mercy on us and bless us."

DISCUSSION POINT

In a world where values have faltered and changed, pluralism—that state where every idea finds justification somewhere and every lifestyle has its advocates—reigns. Polarization has followed so that people have moved into groups for and against all these ideas and lifestyles. Events in our lifetime have led to disillusionment and lack of respect for our leaders. Television has put us inside the walls of our homes so that we no longer know our neighbors. We are fragmented, isolated, lonely, profane, and stressed. We have real pressures on our personal lives. Where is peace? Where can life be OK?

In personal interviews, many people with whom I talked did not admit to feeling stressed. But virtually all people said they think others are. While we can think of persons who live strong, peaceful lives, we see the majority dealing with stress of some kind. We see the world as a crazy, mixed-up, out of balance, and stressful place to live.

Identifying Our Stress Stories

In such a world, it's important to identify our own stress stories. What is stress for us? How is it influenced by where we live and who we know and what we have and do? What does it mean in our own particular lives?

Each LIFESEARCH group will be different from others. Your group lives in a certain region, state, and town. It represents a certain age range: young, middle, or older adult, with stage-of-life stresses. Probably it falls into a certain economic bracket and general lifestyle. It is different from another group across town. If you are a group in a large-membership church, it is different from other groups in your local church. Who are you as a group?

What did you learn from developing your group descriptions? Do you feel all the words belong there? Which ones are most influential on how life is for you? Which ones made you feel good? Which ones do you wish could be taken off the list?

GROUP INTERACTION

Add words to your group description that represent the sources of stress in your lives.

DISCUSSION POINT

Talk about your list.

Stressor: An event or condition that may be physical, social, or psychological, including anticipation and imagination, that triggers a stress reaction.

(From Controlling Stress and Tension: A Holistic Approach, *by Daniel A. Girdano and George S. Every; Prentice-Hall, 1986; page 6.)*

WRITTEN REFLECTION

DISCUSSION POINT

You have focused on your group. You have focused on yourself.

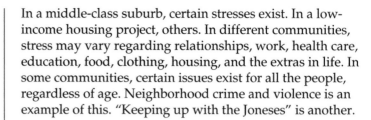

In a middle-class suburb, certain stresses exist. In a low-income housing project, others. In different communities, stress may vary regarding relationships, work, health care, education, food, clothing, housing, and the extras in life. In some communities, certain issues exist for all the people, regardless of age. Neighborhood crime and violence is an example of this. "Keeping up with the Joneses" is another.

Zoom in now on yourself as an individual member of this LIFESEARCH group.

Regardless of what others say, <u>what do you think stress is?</u> Everybody in the group already knows a great deal about it: what it is, how it feels, and how he or she reacts to it. We can learn by taking time out in the midst of life to think more about stress, individually and together.

Complete the following sentences:

1. My definition of stress is . . .

2. I can tell I am stressed when . . .

3. Some ways for dealing with stress are . . .

4. People today are stressed because . . .

5. When stressed, I wish I could . . .

<u>What have you learned so far?</u>

No life is without some stress. Both rich and poor worry about family and friends, work issues, money, health, education, the world, and their own futures. Some people function better under stress. Most know there are different levels of stress and that a certain amount of it is not only okay but good. For example, without a little stage fright, actors do not give their best performance. A marathon runner is under great stress, but she has chosen it for a number of reasons and finds great joy in participating in the marathon.

DISCUSSION POINT

What are the moments of "spirit-breaking" stress in your life?

What were helpful ways of dealing with it?

What do you think about the busy counselor's statement?

Some stress is spirit breaking. It becomes so great that the mind tracks it constantly, the body records its wear and tear, the spirit flags. Some stress is serious enough to require the help of others in dealing with it. Seeking this kind of help shows strength, not weakness. I interviewed a busy counselor who said, "The weak and submissive do not come to me or join my groups. I see the survivors. They are the ones who seek help."

Assess Your Stress Level

With all the studies done on stress, many simple tests and exercises have been designed to allow individuals to assess their own stress levels. Perhaps the best known is the Holmes-Raye Life Event Survey. Life events such as the death of a loved one, a change in jobs, a mortgage, trouble in a relationship, an outstanding personal achievement are listed with points attached to each. After persons mark their life events, they add up their points. People are often surprised to realize how high their score is. At the survey's end, a simple analysis leads people to consider what they should do to take care of themselves while dealing with their issues.

Contact your area hospital's wellness or stress center for information about the Holmes-Raye Life Event Survey.

WRITTEN REFLECTION

On a separate piece of paper, write down your own major life events and changes for the past two years. These may be related to your family, friends, work, church, outside activities, health, finances. They may be about difficulties, but if there were peak experiences such as winning an award, being given a promotion, or holding an office, put these down as well. Positive things can be stressful, too.

GROUP INTERACTION

As an optional activity, distribute chenille strips (pipe cleaners) to group members. Ask them to bend their strips to indicate major life events of the last two years. Allow time for group members to share their "stress indicator" with a partner and/or the whole group.

DISCUSSION POINT

Review your "major events" exercise. What helped you manage your stress?

DISCUSSION POINT

BIBLE STUDY

After allowing time for group members to read Ephesians 4:1-16 individually, ask persons to share the words they identified. Ask which words from this Bible passage might have special personal meaning for dealing with stress.

On the continuum below, picture where you think you belong at this time in your life. Where would you have pictured yourself six months ago? Two years ago?

Low stress									**High stress**	
0	1	2	3	4	5	6	7	8	9	10

What can this exercise tell us? We may learn quite a bit! As we track the major life events of the past two years, we may have confirmed that we were quite distressed! For example, one individual identified that in one eight-week period she (1) received a special-needs child through a "whirlwind" adoption placement, (2) moved to a new home over a thousand miles away, (3) changed from a demanding professional position to a challenging stay-at-home lifestyle as a mother and homemaker, (4) grieved the loss of a supportive community of friends and colleagues, and (5) purchased a new home.

What did we learn from living through stress? We may learn that we can handle stressful periods by developing strong coping skills. We may need to take extra care with ourselves for a while. We may want to plan a change in activities or attitude, more relaxation, more healthful food, more time for ourselves, or other things we think will work for us.

Spiritual Resources

In my interviews to explore how people view and handle stress, older adults usually mentioned spiritual resources. Adults below their mid-40's seldom did. How do you feel about this? What are some reasons you think this happened? Can the church help younger adults develop earlier awareness of the resources of prayer and spirituality, whatever life brings?

The Bible speaks often of stressful times. A favorite passage of many people is Ephesians 4:1-16. Read this passage. Look for special words of strength and guidance. Watch for words that show Paul knew about the thing we now call stress.

GROUP INTERACTION

Lead the group in trying this experiment.

What message about your own life and spirit do you get from this simple experiment?

WRITTEN REFLECTION

BEFORE NEXT TIME

WORSHIP

Take a moment to explore your stress. Are you aware that your body keeps a running score of your stress points? Drop your head forward onto your chest. Do you feel any tightness anywhere? Take a deep breath. Relax your shoulders. Slowly drop your head forward again.

Now tighten a fist. Is your mind, your body, your life like this at times? When? Loosen your fist. Open your palm. Breathe deeply. Clench your fist quickly. Gently loosen it. Let your hand lie gently on your lap. Breathe deeply.

Whatever your stress load and however well or poorly you are carrying it at the moment, breathe deeply again. Know that this breath of life is the closest sign you have that God loves you beyond your understanding and always will. God sees the stress and difficulty in your life and stands waiting to help you carry that load and maybe even put it down. God sees this in every person seated in your midst.

As this study begins, spend several moments identifying your personal goals for this study. What goals do you have about the stress in your life? Write them below:

Choose a specific goal for the coming week and name it aloud.

As you prepare to close the session, write prayer concerns of your group members in the space below:

Pray this prayer or one in your own words:

Loving Creator of those before you now, bless each one of us, living life in a stress-prone world. Help us remember it is not stress but our response to it that counts the most. Help us see that through your love we can be no longer children, tossed to and fro and blown about by every wind, but may grow in Christ, adults at peace with ourselves and the world. Bless us in the week ahead. Help us to take good care of ourselves. Help us to meet others and life's events in a way that meets your hopes for us. Guide us as we think and pray about the stress in our lives. In our brother Jesus' name and for your glory, we pray. Amen.

CHAPTER TWO

JUST TALKING HELPS

"There is a real yearning for community in our culture. I think that is one of the reasons you see so many different types of support groups. . . . It is too bad that . . . you often have to have an illness or an addiction before you can become a part of a community. But if you talk with people, the community really helps . . . because it fulfills that deeper need."

(From *Healing and the Mind*, by Bill Moyers; Doubleday, 1993; page 107.)

At a late Saturday lunch, the thirty-year-old talked about stress. She had played in an "ultimate Frisbee tournament" in 100-degree heat. The games lasted longer than she expected, making her stressed over her late arrival at lunch. She was studying for qualifying exams for her Ph.D. She was selling her house. She was moving to a new city and a new job in a month. A person who takes church membership seriously, she said some plain things about the church's unwillingness to have people's real problems brought inside it. She discredited the church for wanting everybody to tithe time, talent, and money, and not rock the boat. The question was asked, "If the church could do anything to help you with stress, what would you like it to do?" After a long moment, she said, "Just talking about it helps. Maybe the church could just provide opportunities to talk about it."

DISCUSSION POINT

If the church could help you, what kind of help would you want with your own stress?

A gifted young minister listened intently. He had been appointed to begin a new church that was moving fast in its first summer program. He was working on knowing his limits and knowing when to let go. One son had just had surgery for a birth condition. The other had been diagnosed with Attention Deficit Disorder. The minister was facing major surgery himself in a week. One could imagine the load being carried by his fine young working wife. <u>The question to him: "If you were going to sit down with others at church to talk about stress, what would you like to talk about?" His eyes looked reflective. "Am I different? Is my stress the same or different from theirs? How does my stress level compare? And how does my stress level affect others?"</u>

What Would You Like to Know?

Q: If the church could help you, what kind of help would you want with your own stress?

A: The church could help by teaching me a new stress response, a concrete response like putting my foot on the brake when a car pulls in front of me, an automatic response for when stress suddenly crops up. How can I put on the brakes in my life? The church could help instill self-worth. The church could talk to persons about their value. If we could really believe in our innate value, we might not be trapped so easily by what stresses us.

In a series of interviews I conducted to write this book, no one said, "Give me a lot of scientific research, especially statistics."

No one said, "Print a lot of footnoted references about the subject."

No one said, "I want to be an expert on stress in general and be educated enough to teach others all about it."

They all said, in essence, "I'd like to get personal and talk about how it is for me and how it is for other people. Just talking about it helps."

<u>Are you like them?</u>

DISCUSSION POINT

Imagine that the writer interviewed you. What do you hope to get out of this study?

So you don't want to know that Hans Selye, great pioneer in the vast work on stress, chose references from 80,000 titles available in the library of his institute in the 1930's when he did his research and wrote his books? You don't care about all the books written since?

DISCUSSION POINT

Do you agree with these observations? Why or why not?

You don't want to know that contemporary psychotherapist Ann Wilson Schaef, in her book *Beyond Therapy, Beyond Science* (HarperCollins, 1992), says that the majority of therapists supposedly helping us deal with our problems are codependent on us? You don't want to know that she believes that we should not adjust to the stress we live with today but instead resist it in order to make the world a better place to live?

You don't want to know what Charles Swindoll, in his book *The Grace Awakening* (Word, 1990), tells about today's evangelical movement against rigidity of belief and against persons setting themselves up as judge and jury, and spouting do's and don'ts to the rest of the world?

Of course I could not resist telling you. From the stacks of books around me, I chose to report those three observations for these reasons:

(1) Stress is a serious issue for caregivers. We know that too many people are sick and dying in their body, mind, and spirit from their inability to respond in healthy ways to stress. We know what causes stress and our personal responses to stress. At its worst, unmanaged wear and tear uses us up. At best, unmanaged stress forms us into persons we do not necessarily want to be.

DISCUSSION POINT

Has unmanaged stress used up any part of your body, mind, or spirit? Has it formed you into something or someone you don't necessarily want to be?

DISCUSSION POINT

(2) Schaef's idea that we should not cope with particular stress but rather eliminate it from the world, an idea countless others are promoting, may be a critical idea for today. We have accepted many harmful premises, practices, and purposes without thinking about them. We have bought a bill of goods about what success, achievement, and maturity are about. Who has sold us this bill of goods? What makes us get on the treadmill, run when it speeds up, and move into the fast lane if we can? Where does it end?

(3) As for Swindoll, I may not agree with him on everything, but—to use an old southern expression—I'd like to hug his neck. He is such a lover of people. His energy, ideas, and commitment pour off the pages of his books. I am hungry to be fed in the Spirit, and I long for Christian community with all kinds of believers. Yet some of the most dedicated Christians I have known in recent years were as stressed as they could be by their spiritual housekeeping of the world. And I have been stressed (mildly, to be sure) by feeling that I could never live up to what they thought I should be and do.

No shortage exists of stiff-necked Christians. Conservatives are not the only ones with strict ideas about others. Liberals, too, get uppity and judgemental. It's no fun! Hooray for Chuck Swindoll!

Now, back to what YOU want to talk about!

Issue One: Just talking about stress helps.

Issue Two: Am I different? How does my stress level compare with and affect others?

Issue Three: How can I put on the brakes?

Below are questions for discussion designed to help you focus on your stress issues.

1. Name two situations that cause you stress.

2. Choose one of those situations to discuss.

3. Describe the most recent time this situation was stressful to you. What happened? What did you do, how did you act, and how did you feel when the episode was over?

4. What worries you about stress?

5. Are you better or worse at handling stress than you were five years ago? Explain.

6. Do you get more stressed at certain times of the year? If so, when and why?

7. Is some of your stress related to the family in which you grew up? If so, explain.

8. Have you outgrown some stresses and developed new ones at this stage in your life?

9. How do you feel your stress level compares with the stress level of others?

10. How do you feel your stress level affects others? Who do you think it affects most?

11. How does stress affect your body? your mind? your spirit?

12. If you could change yourself to deal with stress better, what changes would you make?

"Stress is more than an isolated incident: it is the product of an entire lifestyle."

(From Controlling Stress and Tension: A Holistic Approach, *by Daniel A. Girdano and George S. Every, Jr.; Prentice-Hall, 1986; page xvi.*)

Listen to what some average people said as they reflected on how stress affects them.

A thirty-seven-year-old owner of a popular barbecue restaurant, when asked if he ever felt stressed, gave a quick sidelong look to see if I were serious, then broke into a half laugh, and said, "Every day." A corporate executive the same age laughed and said, "Maybe God invented stress to let us know when we're off track!"

The majority of people said, "Too much to do, too little time." A number talked about living up to others' expectations. One woman in her mid-thirties talked about how life has changed since she was a child: "When I was little, nobody's mother worked outside the home. Perhaps one or two had a mother who taught school. But now, not only do all the mothers work outside the home, but everybody is expected to work. Not only are you expected to work, with the cost of everything, no one has any choice. It seems as though, in each decade, life leaps forward a little more—leap, leap, leap—until here we are. Everybody's running around all the time, working, needing more money, going into debt. Would I go back to the way things were? Yes!" Another woman said, "Sometimes I long to go back. . . to grow my own food."

Still others said, "What about the future? Jobs? The economy? Everybody has a beeper. Everybody has a car phone. It's not healthy! Some people drink, smoke, spend too much money dealing with stress. We're oversaturated with information! Fast food is not fast enough. Pizza delivery is within thirty minutes or free! Everything is twenty-four-hour service, open on Sunday. I worry about my clients, that I can't do what they want. I worry about meeting the payroll. I worry about downsizing. What do they mean, right-sizing? Where does that leave me? I'd like to ignore a lot of things, but I can't. I can't sit still. I can't go to sleep at first. Something drives me to keep up, even when I don't believe in it. At my age there is still peer pressure, but it is about different things. Everybody's busy all the time. 'Busy' is a status symbol! AAUGH!"

DISCUSSION POINT

Discuss each of these possibilities as producing stress for our time.

How did we get this way? Here are some possibilities.

One man said, "The electric light was invented, and we could stay up all night. That did it!"

As people have become better educated, anything has seemed possible. After World War II, peace and prosperity ensued. People made more money and acquired more than they needed of just about everything. Wealth has created a life where even the extras are affordable, and people have them.

Television has made us a global village in which everybody can see what is going on all over the world, what everyone has, and therefore what is "in" and desirable. We have bought it. We have stayed inside new air conditioned houses and watched television and lost our connections with others. We have money to buy good cars, eat out all the time, and run up credit card bills.

Somewhere about the time of the Vietnam War, cynicism and skepticism arrived, first about our country, then about our institutions. This reality is an undertow with which we have not completely come to terms. It keeps up a low hum of stress in Americans who once thought their country was number one and always would be. Disagreement over how to manage our superpower has split us into what becomes ugly divisions at times. The speed of life and the threat of our differences have put strains on our most normal, ordinary relationships.

A professional counselor said, "I don't know what we are going to have to do to get people to slow down. Most people confuse activity with success. The more places you go, the better you are. We say, 'I have been there. I bought that. I have a CD player' (even though we don't have time to listen to it). Many persons seem to confuse activity with pleasure. People think they have to be accomplished in all areas and that they have to have everything. Just because you write everything down on your calendar does not mean you are in control of your life."

DISCUSSION POINT

Do you agree? Why? Why not?

In our affluent culture, even Christians forget that others are stressed because they do not have enough to eat or a decent place to live, because they cannot afford to get sick. We live detached lives, deliberately unaware, defensive of our right to keep what we have, believing our possessions are security.

BIBLE STUDY

Read Isaiah 58:6-14. <u>How does reading it affect you?</u>

DISCUSSION POINT

Do you want similar things?

<u>Here's how it affected me: It made me say, "Yes. Yes, this is what I want. This is how I want things to be. I want to share myself and my life with others without fear. I want my light to break forth and my healing to spring up. I want the Lord to guide me. I want to be like a watered garden. I want to have the ruins rebuilt, to be called the repairer of the breach, to restore my city's streets."</u>

GROUP INTERACTION

In smaller groups of two or three persons, discuss how reading Isaiah 58:6-14 affects you.

Read Isaiah 58:6-14. Be aware that in a world like ours, one's sabbath may not come on a Sunday. It is simply "a day apart," (maybe Tuesday, maybe Thursday) for the ordering of life, for the blessing and empowering of the other six days. It may be the day we take to remember what life is about. The concept of sabbath rest may also nudge us to live daily life in rhythm and balance—work, worship, leisure, and service included.

DISCUSSION POINT

What if we did honor, once more, sabbath rest? What do you think it would do for your stress level? What is it that really keeps you from doing it?

BEFORE NEXT TIME

Try observing sabbath rest one day during this coming week. Really observe a sabbath. Think about what you want sabbath to mean in your life. In addition to rereading Isaiah 58:6-14, you might also contemplate Genesis 2:1-3, Exodus 20:8-11, Deuteronomy 5:12-15, and Matthew 12:1-14. Plan ahead how you will observe the sabbath so that it will truly be sabbath for you.

WORSHIP

Awareness is growing that we have veered from the path God intended for us. A parade is forming of persons choosing to walk to the Original Drummer, catching the hands of those who stand on the sidelines and drawing them in to share the day in a more livable world.

As you end this session, invite group members to share some of their personal joys and concerns or those of the world. Record them in the space below.

Pray this prayer or another one in your own words.

Dear God, may we meet you in the midst of our lives, that you may set us free, heal us, and enable us to be strong and clear. Set us on track once again, in touch with what life is all about. Life is good, Lord. Help us to live it according to your will. In Jesus' name, Amen.

CHAPTER THREE

NO STRESS IN MY RELATIONSHIPS, PLEASE!

CHECKING IN

As you begin this session, invite group members to share what has happened in their lives since the last time you met. Invite them particularly to share about victories in handling the stress they find in their lives.

DISCUSSION POINT

Consider the walls that have been created in your life. Are some walls gifts? barriers?

DISCUSSION POINT

Who are the people who inspire your trust?

Who are the persons who provide you rest and refreshment?

A beautiful young girl sat on the rug in front of the sofa. Around the room other young people sat on furniture and on the floor. They sought a theme for their youth ministry. This meeting was one of the deep, probing meetings held each fall when it fell to a new group to choose the next year's theme. Everyone knew this girl had been through great suffering with the sudden, tragic death of her father and the difficult events that followed. The discussion was about breaking down walls. She said, "You know, sometimes walls are gifts. If I hadn't built a wall between myself and a couple of other people in the last few years, I wouldn't have survived. My wall protected me, and gave me space and time to heal."

An employee, commenting about a colleague, said, "I thought she wouldn't get to me again. I have learned to stay away from her. I try not to ask her to help me with anything. I only go to her when I have to. I go in braced for her to be negative and to put me down. It's not right, but I am used to her undercuts and just pass them off. I can't get involved every time that happens. Still, sometimes I have to ask her something. It happened again today. She made one of those responses and it was like my house of cards came tumbling down. Suddenly I was angry, with no place to put it. I have to work with her. But it's a real drag and probably influences how I feel about my job as much as any other single thing. I'm a Christian, but I'm no good at handling this situation. What am I going to do?"

He stood there in the sunshine in his big, flat-brimmed hat and laughed as he looked down at the crowd around him. A professional storyteller, he saw deep into the hard times and secrets of his heroes and heroines: working poor, family members with painful flaws, little boys in trouble. Through his telling of their struggles, their nobility emerged. People flocked to his performances and enjoyed standing near him, at leisure, on this sun-decked morning. In a world grown crowded and disillusioned, he inspired their trust. The crowd found rest and refreshment.

DISCUSSION POINT

Which statement more accurately matches your experience?

BIBLE STUDY

In smaller groups of two to four persons, scan through the Gospel accounts in the Bible and identify those persons with whom Jesus cultivated a personal relationship.

Ask: How did Jesus benefit from his human relationships?

How do you benefit from the relationships you have with others?

BIBLE STUDY

Read the Bible passages referred to in the main text. Discuss the feelings group members think Jesus must have felt in those circumstances.

The humorist Will Rogers once said he never met a man he didn't like.

Down through the years, people have said, "He just didn't know some of the folks I know."

Engaging the Scriptures

Without question, in the Gospel writings, we see how important relationships were to Jesus. Jesus spent valuable time, not just teaching and healing the "masses," but in developing close friendships with men, women, and children. I still remember the moment when I read an interpretation on Luke 24:50. The reading pointed out that Jesus' ascension took place relatively near the home of his friends, Mary, Martha, and Lazarus. Who knows, perhaps he might have stopped off to see these dear friends on his way? The speculation reminded me of Jesus' deep humanity and his need for others. Could Jesus need anything? Some will say Jesus could not. He was the Son of God, the Savior of the world.

Jesus did not want to go it alone. Community and relationships were vitally important to him. Initially he chose twelve disciples to help him change the world. He wanted to be with them.

He had parents he loved, and his carpenter father taught him a trade. At least once he went his own way, much to his parents' complaint: "Child, why have you treated us like this? Look, your father and I have been searching for you in great anxiety" (Luke 2:48). "But they did not understand what he said to them" (50).

Mark 6:1-6 packs the pain of hometown relationships into six sad verses. In the group of twelve with whom he spent most of his time, one betrayed him for money (Mark 14:10-11) and one of the strongest denied knowing him in his greatest moment of loneliness and suffering (Mark 14:66-72). On the cross, he gave his mother and John, a beloved disciple, to each other because Jesus loved Mary and wanted to know she would be cared for (John 19:25b-27).

His openness to persons would make him seem quite sophisticated today. He truly was open to all and lived inclusively. He was confrontational when necessary. He was confronted, himself, time and again, by those who feared him. He lived in close, direct relationship with individuals and crowds. He handled his own stressful moments by getting away alone to pray. Jesus knows firsthand what we are talking about when we talk to him about relationships. <u>Remember, his last stop was Bethany.</u>

The Journey Inward

Relationships with others are so important that sometimes we do not realize the greatest relational stress we have is our relationship with ourselves. We do not believe in ourselves. We do not trust that who we are is good enough. The adage, "Just be yourself," falls on deaf ears, because we find it too hard or scary. "If I am just myself, if they see who I really am, they will not like me." So we pretend, try too hard or not enough, hide our feelings, do not say what we honestly think or believe, and are worn out and lonely, sometimes even in the heart of our families. Sometimes, after long being covered with layers of masks and hoped-for acceptability, we will say, "Well, who am I, anyway? It has been so long since I felt free to be myself, I don't know who I am or what is really important to me. I just want to be loved and accepted. It doesn't really matter who I am."

In the space below, reflect on who you are. Try to appraise yourself honestly.

Thinking about what we need and reaching out for it is a healthy thing to do. It matters who you are. It matters what you think, what you need, and what you want to give and receive. Maybe the one intimate trustworthy relationship, that universal first choice, does not fall into place. Many other ways exist to love and be loved. Mother Teresa is one of the more recent examples of a totally fulfilled single individual. But there are people living alone in your own church and

DISCUSSION POINT

Where would your "last stop" be if you knew yourself to be facing death? Why?

WRITTEN REFLECTION

DISCUSSION POINT

Can you think of examples of such individuals in your community?

community whose lives have been lived in beautiful service to others. They have chosen something unselfish to do. Their lives count. Their cups run over.

Too many people are walking around with low self-esteem. This inner condition has more influence on their relationship stories than they know. If this rings true for you, do not discount it. Begin to pray about it in earnest. Talk with someone you trust.

The Journey Outward

Categories of relationships exist in every life: the family in which one is raised; spousal, parent/child, blended family, friend, sibling, peers at work, manager/employee, church folk, club and organization, even public strangers. Add to my list if you like. Begin to think of types of stress that occur in these relationships.

In the space provided, write down not less than three and not more than five of your personal relationships. These may be current or past relationships. Your list may include relationships with persons who are dead or alive, for relationships continue to affect us, positively or negatively, throughout life. Consider which relationships have been most critical to you.

Rank them in the space provided at the top of page 25, with 1 being most likely to raise stress levels and the last number being the least likely.

Visualize your relationships as ranked. If you think the other person or persons in that relationship primarily brings (brought) stress on you, put a check under "The Other Person." If you think you primarily bring (brought) stress on them, check under "Me."

DISCUSSION POINT

As a group, make a general list of the types of stress that might occur in the relationships mentioned in the main text.

WRITTEN REFLECTION

WRITTEN REFLECTION

Relationship	The Other Person	Me

1.

2.

3.

4.

5.

GROUP INTERACTION

Invite group members to share briefly with a neighbor. Encourage persons to avoid using the names of real people who are not present. If names are necessary, be careful of the persons they represent. They cannot defend themselves.

GROUP INTERACTION

Invite group members quickly to choose one relationship from their list for the purpose of analysis and roleplay. In small groups of two, three, or four persons, first discuss the questions listed under "A. For the Analysis" in the main text.

A. For the Analysis:

1. Identify the root causes of stress in this relationship.

2. When and how does this stress usually arise?

3. What happens then?

4. Who usually does the most to decrease the stress?

5. Can stress sometimes be good for a relationship?

6. What resources do people in this relationship have for making things better or worse?

7. Do they usually use these resources?

GROUP INTERACTION

Next, ask members of the smaller groups to take turns following the instructions under "B. For the Roleplay" in the main text.

B. For the Roleplay:

1. Identify a specific time when this relationship might become stressful.

2. Ask two (or more) people to volunteer to play the parts in the relationship.

3. Help the roleplayers stay focused on the relationship itself and not on a particular situation surrounding it. This may be hard but it will be worth it.

GROUP INTERACTION

Still within the smaller groups, ask persons to follow the instructions under "C. For the Debriefing."

C. For the Debriefing:

1. Thank the roleplayers. They risked themselves and need your support.

2. Without judging or blaming, state your observations of what happened. What did you see? What did you hear?

3. How did you feel about what happened between the two?

4. Did you sympathize or empathize with one or the other?

5. What did you learn from this roleplay?

Remember that everyone in the group has experiences, thoughts, feelings, and opinions of their own. Be sensitive to this. Get involved. But refrain from talking too long. Do not interrupt others. Gate keep: take responsibility for enabling each person to get a chance to talk. Do not interpret what others say to the rest of the group. Ask them what they mean, if you do not know. Let them speak for themselves. If you disagree, say so, but respect the viewpoint of any speaker. Remember that the time is short. Be willing to move on.

Keeping an Eye on the Ball

Is there anyone alive who does not have at least one other person with whom he or she clashes, differs to the extreme, or simply has difficulty in getting along?

A friend walked into my office and began to read the material on my wall. Cartoons, pictures, and quotes I want to see are pinned up. I also have a copy of an ad from the paper. In the foreground is a baseball, in the background, a bat leaning against a wall. The legend says, "Keep your eye on the ball."

I said, "Everything I see these days speaks to my writing project. The thing with the ball is about my book."

"How so?" he asked.

I told him, another Christian, some of my thoughts about relationships. I thought that when anyone hurts our feelings, we want to hurt them in return. When anyone is rude, we want to get even. When people brutally try to dominate us, we want to shrink them down to size and sometimes try to do so with derogatory comments behind their backs. At times like that, if you "keep your eye on the ball," a Christian can remember the person he or she wants to be and behave accordingly, no matter what the other person has done or said.

My friend said, "That's hard."

I said, "But it's what it's all about, isn't it?"

"Yes," he said, "that really is what it's all about."

Many of us pass on our stress to others, whoever they may be, family, friends, or even strangers behind a counter or in another car. We get so full of fatigue or tension from the momentum of the day, we unload mindlessly. We meet others, full of complaints. We yell, or shove the dog, shifting our load to the innocent.

A powerful young executive spoke of the moment before he went in the door at home at night to his wife and three children. He said, "If I can remember to pray, if I can pray in time, it makes all the difference in the world."

I said, "What do you pray for?"

He said, "To serve my family."

He told a story he had heard a minister tell on a radio program. He said, "This old preacher was a terrific storyteller. He really got into it, and he had this wonderful voice and deep southern accent. In his sermon, he began talking about his wife of many years and what a saint she was. He told several stories on himself, when his wife could have really scalded him for what he had done or how he had acted. But every time, she came up with a gentle response or support and encouragement. At the end of each little story, the preacher in his rolling voice would say, 'She could have broken my spirit, but she. . .'"

She was a woman who kept her eye on the ball!

WORSHIP

Ask the group members to listen to the Bible passages read aloud and to respond to each one with the words, "Keep your eye on the ball."

As you near the end of this chapter, undergird your study with Scripture. Read aloud 1 Peter 2:9-10 and 1 Peter 3:8-11.

Close this session with sentence prayers for yourselves and for each other, or use the prayer printed below.

Dear God, bless us when we struggle to find our way in our relationships. Help us keep our eye on the ball of who we want to be, for you and others, even when we are caught in stressful times with them. Help us see ourselves more clearly and the ways we bring stress to others. When we are tired or tense, help us pray in time. When we are angry or upset, help us never to break another person's spirit. Teach us, through everyone we meet, positive or negative, to be more gentle, to be more kind. Teach us to be more patient and to see beyond the moment to the cause of a stressful problem. By your Spirit, lead us to be more loving, God. Because of your mercy to us, help us be merciful to others. We beg you this. In Jesus' name. Amen.

CHAPTER FOUR

NO ONE SAID LIFE WOULD BE EASY

CHECKING IN

As you begin the session, invite group members to share high and low points of their lives since your last session. Invite them specifically to share areas of stress in their lives and how they are handling those areas.

She had no idea how beautiful a Christian she was as she sat in the *Disciple* group that Sunday afternoon and said, "He had not been able to walk unaided for some time, but he always wanted to get up and go to the bathroom. I would put one of his arms around my shoulder and, holding him with one arm around his waist, we would go. Sometimes he was so weak he could hardly move, and I would put one foot behind his and shove his feet forward one at a time. He had fallen several times and I could hardly get him up. I just wasn't strong enough. It took everything I had and sometimes took a long time for us to get him back to bed. I loved him so much. I would have done anything for him, and I was really trying. But I was so tired. This particular night had been so hard. He was finally back in the bed. I walked out on the front porch and stood there looking up at the sky. I said, 'Lord, I've done just about all I can. I am worn out now. I just have to place him in your hands for your will to be done.' In a couple of days, he died. This may not be right, but I have always thought God let me keep him as long as we could make it, but when I couldn't do any more, God took him home. And I really feel good in knowing that I did everything I could for him."

It was a national annual amputee sports tournament. A swimmer with no hands raced through her lane. A man with no legs from the hips down turned the wheels strongly as he raced in his wheelchair. One who lost his legs at the knees in a work-related accident ran swiftly on artificial legs. The fleeting sound bite on television said, "They don't inspire pity. They just inspire."

A Christian educator said, "The most stressed people I know are young working mothers. They do everything for everybody, including their church."

An employee reflected, "At work, the atmosphere is tough. We look nice and civilized. But there are all these undercurrents. Cliques exist. I guess every office has people who jockey for position. It gets old. Sometimes during the day I catch myself staring at the wall, wondering what I'm doing here. I remember a teaching from church about my value as a per-

DISCUSSION POINT

Ask group members if there are any points in the main text or sidebars so far that they want to discuss.

son, and I think about that. The only thing that could be worse about my job would be losing it. Remembering that fact gets my gratitude going. I don't know what I would do without my church friends. They really mean a lot."

Another woman whom I interviewed narrowed her eyes a bit in thought. Then she said, "What makes it stress is that there is nothing in between me and it."

Listen to the voices of others, all interviewed as I researched the nature of stress. Stressful situations happen: family illness; loss of a job; destructive weather; an aging parent or one with Alzheimer's; one's own illness; death of a loved one; divorce; debt; addiction to a substance or work or a person; change in location or personal habits; holidays; problems of race, gender, sex; a friend with AIDS; too much to do, too little time.

Every situation has its own story. This or that is different. But the competitive spirit and the culture we live in create high-voltage pressures on relationships, families, school performance, work, even leisure time. "Are we as open as they are? Can we talk about everything?" "Are the kids making A's and getting in the right clubs?" "Will he make the team?" "If I get any more work to do, I'll scream." "No one cares about the stress level in this department." "If I have to take care of all this stuff this weekend, when will I ever just rest?"

While we live, all of us have the same amount of time. God seems to think it is good for the sun and the moon to appear in certain rhythms. People tell time by them, but we are still learning how to use it. How much is possible (or not possible) to put into a day? What is reasonable for us to do in terms of stamina and temperament? And what is really worth doing? Is there time for burning the candle at both ends or for smelling the flowers? And how do we achieve a balance?

Even too much fun can produce stress as it becomes not fun at all. For example, many Americans attempt to do too many things on vacation. We eat, drink, and spend too much. We forget that life has limits!

Reflect on Your Stresses

A fairly large circle has been provided for this experience. The circle represents you—or another a human being, if you prefer.

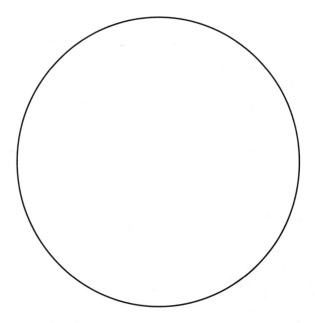

1. Outside the circle, write words or draw pictures of everyday situations that cause you stress (for instance, constant deadlines and work load).

2. Inside the circle, list inner individual characteristics that add to the stress of these situations (for instance, a short temper, lack of aptitude, or positive values such as honesty). Be specific. Name the aptitude or the values that add to your present stressful situation.

3. Draw arrows outside the circle pointing in, and arrows inside the circle pointing out, a way of illustrating stress.

4. If you believe anything you have diagrammed could be changed, put a question mark by it.

5. Study what you have done. Decide your own greatest need in this situation and write it at the bottom of the page.

6. Before you share your work with a partner, pray. Focus your prayer on your greatest need.

DISCUSSION POINT

7. Share your work with one other person. Then share briefly in the total group.

DISCUSSION POINT

To what extent do you agree with the writer's statement?

BEFORE NEXT TIME

Try this "color bath" experience sometime during the coming week.

DISCUSSION POINT

Discuss the questions in the main text. In addition, ask:

To what extent have you been too proud to accept help as suggested in the main text?

What is the worst that might happen if you were to swallow your pride and reach for such help?

In what ways would that "worst" case be worse than the stress you already feel?

Coping With Life as It Is

In a newspaper column on work, the writer spoke of people who were unhappy in their work but were unable to find other jobs. He said, "If you've tried everything you can to change the situation, you cannot get out of it, and you are still unhappy, get happy. Change your attitude." It may not be a bad suggestion. Not always, but sometimes, it may also be the best Christian response.

Regardless of the focus of the situation, finding zones in which to live one's life also works. Carve out time to stop, reflect on something positive, remember you are God's creature, and pray. These are time-honored ways to cope with life as it is.

Carve out two hours just to play. Go to a mall and take a color bath. Color lifts our spirits. Malls are full of color. They are warm or cool, as the season calls for. Walking is good. Walking through malls is like taking a color bath. Color baths are on my recommended stress-breaker list, and they're free!

A reader with an ill family member may say to herself, "I could never get away to play." Before she accepts this idea, she should be sure there is no support group or person in her church willing to offer relief two hours a week. This valuable assistance is worth arranging. She should never be too proud to accept help. In a growing number of communities around the country, organized support for caregivers is available. It may be critical to her own health. But she may have to swallow her pride and reach out for it.

In your church, is there an organized group to support caregivers? If not, is this a good time to start one?

DISCUSSION POINT

On a scale of one to ten, with ten being the highest, how close would you say you are to being "too busy"?

How does your busyness affect your stress?

If you could let go today of one thing in your life that increases your stress-increasing busyness, what would it be? Why would you choose that?

DISCUSSION POINT

Besides discussing the questions found in the main text, ask: What do you think of the statement, "The church is the greatest source of stress I have"?

To what extent is that statement true for you?

Too Much Good

What about when life itself becomes a stressful situation? You love your family and friends, have a good job, participate in sports or clubs, are active in your church. You would not give up a thing, but you are TOO BUSY! You've "got it all together," but it turns out there is too much of it. It is all good, but there is too much of it. You want it all. It looks great from a distance. But there is too much of it.

Does the church let us go easily if we need to step back from our activities? Two or three people whom I interviewed said, "The church is the greatest source of stress I have. They want me to do it all!" What do we want from our church community in not only helping us with a particular stress but also allowing us to maintain balance in our lives?

Releasing Emotion

As I was writing this session, twenty young people and adults left Birmingham to spend four days in the rain forest in Brazil and ten days on a work experience with a missionary to Brazil. A problem developed when they got to Miami: they had no international tickets because the travel agent had not handled the purchase properly. As we worked agonizingly to rectify the situation, I kept seeing Rachel's face. She is an ardent environmentalist, a teenager already useful to the world just by being in it. She was beaming when she boarded the plane in Birmingham. In Miami she was crestfallen. Rachel's time in the rain forest was being cut short by every hour she was delayed in getting there. While she put the work camp experience first, I knew how much being in the rain forest meant to her.

As we toiled away on the telephone, my enormous anger at the travel agent rose again and again. This experience of unexpected crisis for loved ones brought to my mind the importance of venting feelings when situations become overwhelming. When the wise young man facing surgery said, "I own my feelings," he was a model for us all.

DISCUSSION POINT

In what ways do you think the church taught you that it was inappropriate to become angry or to have negative feelings?

Do the statements in the main text reflect your experience?

DISCUSSION POINT

What do you think when you encounter a person who is this open and honest about his or her feelings?

DISCUSSION POINT

If you were to own your feelings at this moment, how would you describe what those feelings are?

BIBLE STUDY

Read Romans 8:18-39 in several translations. Ask:

How do different translations portray Romans 8:28?

How do you understand Romans 8:28?

Somewhere along the way the church taught many of us it was not nice to be angry or have negative feelings. However well-intentioned, the church did us no favors with this mistaken idea. Today the church is filled with people who do not know what to do with the feelings they have. They fool themselves. Sometimes they are able to fool others. They try to be something they cannot be: superhuman.

We need people to model for us how to be human, not how to be superhuman. Christians can model effective ways to handle anger, hostility, resentment, and other feelings. Feelings are part of God's gift of life to us. They help us keep our balance in living. We have negative feelings when something of value to us is threatened. Healthy defenses are alerted. If we abort the process too frequently, something happens inside us that diminishes our possibilities. Healthy ways of dealing with feelings exist, beginning with acknowledging them. Dealing with feelings, especially for Christians, it seems, is a hard lesson to learn. We avoid it at our peril.

Do you know someone who is able to be himself or herself by simply saying, "I don't want to do that," or, "I don't believe that," or "I'm sorry, but I have all I can handle at the moment"? Such persons find themselves able to say, "That makes me angry," or "That hurts my feelings."

There is a special power about a human being's honesty and dignity when the person is speaking directly from his or her center. If the statement comes in the right spirit, the person is accepted and respected. Owning your feelings, speaking honest and directly, and being yourself are high on the list for dealing with the stressful situations of our lives.

Everything . . . for Good?

God does not want us to endure beyond our strength. God gives us feelings, thoughts, and actions for taking care of ourselves in the sudden storms that come on difficult days.

"We know that all things work together for good for those who love God, who are called according to his purpose" (Romans 8:28). Another way of saying this is, "For those who love God, we know God works for good in everything." Does this understanding match your experience? The apostle Paul encouraged Christians to believe that God is able to transform their difficulties. Although Paul well understood the bitterness of daily trials, Paul believed that God has defeated evil. Evil, then, has lost its power ultimately to defeat those "who love God, who are called according to his purpose." For these persons, God works in each difficult situation to bring something good. God never gives up. God keeps looking for ways to send messages and deeds of love and hope in the worst situations of life. God works for good in everything.

GROUP INTERACTION

Ask persons to recall the situation which they chose to explore previously in this session (page 30). Have group members pair off again with the persons with whom they shared during that earlier activity. In pairs, discuss ways you can see that God has worked or is working for good. Encourage them to be sensitive to the smallest signs.

Sometimes this is easy to believe. Sometimes we can put into words just how we see God doing this in the tough situations of our lives. Other times, we do not look, see, or believe.

WORSHIP

Many thoughts and feelings may have surfaced during this session. Encourage persons to own those feelings as you close this session.

Record prayer concerns of group members in the spaces below.

Pray this prayer or one of your own.

Dear God, tough situations come to all of us. We grow strong in the struggle, if it is done in faith. We need you to be with us. Be merciful to us when we fail. Be merciful when we try to be superhuman people and not just human people. For the victories that come, we give you the praise. We feel your spirit, enabling us to be and to do, in the situations of our lives. Thank you for insights that came in this session. Thank you for Jesus who, more than any other who ever lived, showed us the perfect way to endure tough situations. Amen.

CHAPTER FIVE

MINDING THE STORE

CHECKING IN

As you begin this session, be sure to take time to allow group members to share significant happenings in their lives since the last time you met. Especially share about stressful incidents or periods and how the stress was handled or not handled.

The most important relationship you will ever have is the one you have now with yourself.

(From One Minute for Myself: A Small Investment, A Big Reward, *by Spencer Johnson; William Morrow & Co., Inc., 1985); Introduction.*

Habit is habit, not to be flung out of the window by any, but coaxed downstairs a step at a time.

(From Tragedy of Pudd'n Head Wilson, *by Mark Twain)*

"In one study . . . college students who napped or relaxed daily for up to twenty minutes during the daytime had significantly fewer illnesses than those who did not rest.

(From Life After Stress, *by Martin Shaffer; Plenum Press, 1982; page 59)*

After a long day of silent programming before his terminal, he rolled back his chair, slung on his backpack, and whistling, walked out of his office. He made a couple of turns down the long hall, walked out the door, punched the elevator button, and was soon in his car. *I gotta get outta' here* was his thought. He wanted to see his eighteen-month-old stress breaker, a little girl who looked just like him.

In the woman's restroom on the same floor, a woman changed into exercise clothes. She had sat at another terminal all day, working hard at another detail job. She chatted with others about her day and theirs, about the coming weekend, about her exercise class. She laughed as she told about it costing a dollar to go and nothing if you didn't, and said, "I'm not very good at it, but if I can survive it, I feel great about myself when it's over. I meet three friends there and we go out afterwards and talk for an hour or so." With a grin, she said, "I love it!"

Listen to ways others interviewed reduce stress.

"I have to see what's on CNN, and I have to read through the paper before I go to bed. It gets my mind off whatever is going on with me. I disconnect from my own day and check out the world's day. Usually when I get in bed, I read until I go to sleep. If I really want to sleep, I choose something not too engrossing and a little hard to read, like an article on something I don't know much about. My mind gets unhinged from the structure of my day, just enough to let me drift off. It works for me."

GROUP INTERACTION

As leader, pretend that you are a television interviewer. Go around the group interviewing each person briefly. Ask: "Five sessions into this LIFESEARCH study, how do you handle stress today?"

DISCUSSION POINT

What ways can you name for resisting stress in a healthy manner?

What extra equipment can you name that Christians have in the struggle against stress?

GROUP INTERACTION

Ask group members to fantasize about what life would be like without limits. Discuss: In what ways can you imagine a life without limits adding to your stress?

DISCUSSION POINT

What do you think of this understanding of solitude?

Know the Territory

If you do not love yourself enough, you will never make it. If you do not take care of yourself, the price is high. Your spirit will shrink to the size of a raisin. Your mind will be unable to fetch what is important and to put it on your screen. Your body will be too tense, too tired, or too out-of-shape for the life you want to live.

Stress is here to stay. Ways exist to resist stress in a healthy manner. Christians have extra equipment for the struggle. Potentially life-changing pressure can challenge us to new depths and build strengths that are useful to us and to others rather than harmful. But, as the Music Man says, "You have to know the territory."

What territory is this? Our own bodies, minds, and spirits.

All of us have our limits. Limits are gifts. What would a life be without limits? A nightmare! A never-ending run to exhaustion. But we are given, among many other wise gifts, limits. Those who fail to live within them get really stressed out!

So what can a person do? Learn the limits. Treasure them for what they are, our own life's boundaries. Nurture solitude. It may not be possible to withdraw to a retreat center or other isolated spot, but perhaps you can nurture an inner sense of solitude, not dependent on your physical surroundings. Henri J. M. Nouwen, in his book *Reaching Out: The Three Movements of the Spiritual Life* (Doubleday, 1975; page 25), provides us with spiritual insight:

"The word *solitude* can be misleading. It suggests being alone by yourself in an isolated place. . . .It is understandable that those who seriously try to develop their spiritual life are attracted to places and situations where they can be alone, sometimes for a limited period of time, sometimes more or less permanently. But the solitude that really counts is the solitude of heart; it is an inner quality or attitude that does not depend on physical isolation. On occasion this isolation is necessary to develop this solitude of heart, but it would be sad if we considered this essential aspect of the spiritual life as a privilege of monks and hermits. It seems more important than ever to stress that solitude is one of the human capacities that can exist, be maintained and developed in the center of a big city, in the middle of a large crowd and in the context of a very active and productive life. A man or woman who has developed this solitude of heart is no longer pulled apart by the most divergent stimuli of the surrounding world but is able to perceive and understand this world from a quiet inner center."

Diversion

When times get tough, hang on, breathe, back up and get a better view, keep quiet, slow down, change the scene, and remember who you are. Lighten up, look for the positive ("things could be worse"; "this will soon be over"), and wait. Count to ten. Cast about in your mind for what is really important. Think about what you will do when the moment, the episode, is over. When the time comes, reach for your favorite music or book. Get by yourself or get in touch with people with whom you feel safe. Use a little discipline. Just haul yourself to a stop. And breathe.

Do not do anything you will regret later. Hold your tongue. Shut your mouth. Keep your foot off the accelerator. If you cannot cool down, play "Diversion."

What is "Diversion"? It is a game for getting a person through a difficult time. Picture this: You are full of tears and you do not want to cry at this particular moment. You are afraid and cannot get your mind off your fear. You are angry and do not want to let your temper fly. So you let categories float up in your brain and name three things that belong in each: three long green things; three round yellow things; three square things; three words that have a z in them; three quarterbacks; three kinds of dogs; three books in your house. . . .

Never play "Diversion" for long, only long enough to break the moment and allow you to shift the focus away from your stress. (Once in a hospital hall when my brother was waiting for a CAT scan of his brain, we played it. It worked!)

Stress is such a serious issue that someone out there will scornfully label such a tactic as totally silly and ask, "What about prayer?"

GROUP INTERACTION

Try playing "Diversion" in your group. Begin somewhere in the circle and go around, taking turns. Make up your own categories or use the ones in the main text. Whoever begins the process can assign the next category to the person on the right.

DISCUSSION POINT

When you finish trying "Diversion," ask group members to share other ways they have found for reducing stress.

DISCUSSION POINT

In smaller groups of two or three persons, have group members share information about their prayer life. Ask:

What are some of the gifts of an active prayer life?

What are some of the difficulties in developing an active prayer life?

Jesus believed in prayer. In the midst of his busy days, he rose early in order to pray (Mark 1:35). Far be it for me to put anything before prayer. My relationship with God is the most important thing in my life. But the very ability to make up such a foolish (yet helpful) little game like "Diversion" is part of the life God gives us. Christians are resourceful, creative, humorous, tough, tender people. Hooray! Some gifts are more precious than others. While prayer is a precious gift, I am delighted that God gave us inventiveness, too. I have felt God's embracing love many times when it has come to me to play "Diversion." I believe the Spirit reminds me.

Personal Fitness

As a former adult fitness instructor, I know that exercise is another effective stress reducer. While aerobic exercise—exercise that causes us to breathe more rapidly and take in more oxygen—helps strengthen the cardiovascular system, other ways are equally helpful to the body. These are the slow and smooth approaches. Many programs exist from classes to self-help videos.

The classes I have taught focus on pulling ourselves together and walking briskly to music. Then, using various kinds of music, we work through all parts of the body, moving every joint and stretching every muscle. Some days we spend special time on the lower back, some days the neck and shoulders, or the feet. We do routines, using materials like ropes and balls. We end our session on the floor, lower legs elevated on chair seats. Breathing slowly and deeply, we hear words of personal affirmation.

I have seen executives who come late to class, tight-muscled and frowning, but who leave with totally different looks. One executive said, "I'll be honest. I like the whole class, but I come for those last moments of deep relaxation."

I have seen people live through devastating crises in part because of exercise classes. Amazingly, a man afraid of flying credited the class with his gaining the self-confidence to fly for the first time.

WRITTEN REFLECTION

Some of you are active in regular exercise programs. Others never move if you can help it! Reflect on your level of physical fitness in the spaces that follow:

Discuss written reflections. Ask: In what ways might members of the group help one another with aspects of physical fitness?

1. What do you do for exercise?

2. What have you done to develop healthy eating habits?

3. What would you like to do to change your level of exercise or your eating habits?

GROUP INTERACTION

Conclude your discussion by trying the relaxation exercise described in the main text.

Try this brief exercise for relaxation. Take a deep breath. Stand with your arms loose at your sides. Move your shoulders forward, then lift them and carry them around in full circles. Now move them backward in circles. Then drop your head forward. As you lift your head, BREATHE deeply! Repeat three times.

BEFORE NEXT TIME

Here are some body checks for you to try on your own before the next session. When you are driving your car, notice whether you are tense. Consciously relax. Breathe. When you are standing in line waiting, flex your knees gently, just a little. No one will notice and it will help you be less tired. If your feet and legs hurt, roll your feet to the outside and stand that way for a moment or two.

Pay attention to your breathing. Become aware of how you breath. Train yourself to take a deep breath at the times you instinctively know it would do you good. In any situation, it will lower your stress level.

Once I heard a phone conversation between a radio counselor and a sad person depressed by unmanaged stress. The caller had no energy, but she did have a sense of desperation. She seemed to have no money and no resources. The counselor said, "Here is the best idea I can give you today. When you hang up the phone, get up and start walking inside your house. Just do it. All of us in the therapy business know 'the feet lead the mind.' If you will just get up and walk for ten minutes, you will feel better. I promise." I have always hoped the caller followed that advice.

LIFESEARCH members who want to explore further in the area of comprehensive stress management may want to read *The Stress Solution: An Action Plan to Manage Stress in Your Life*, by Lyle H. Miller and Alma Dell Smith (Pocket Books, 1993). This resource seeks to help persons develop an individual stress management plan.

Fortify Your Spirit

None of this works for you? You are in a stressful time of your life—a problem won't go away, a person deals you misery, a situation is overwhelming? You need a safe place to put this load down. If you can, share your pain with this group. Ask them for their prayers and for suggestions about helpful persons or agencies with whom to share the pressures of this current time. Remember that reaching out for help is not a sign of weakness, but of strength.

And what about fortifying the spirit? Try reading the psalms in the Bible. From the shelves of inspirational books in any bookstore, library, or your pastor's study, get whatever books speak to you at the moment, and read them. Borrow a hymnal from your church. Turn the pages and keep reading until you strike gold—it is there. Or go and sit silently in the sanctuary of your church, eyes on the altar. Just wait. Just sit there and wait, believing.

GROUP INTERACTION

In smaller groups with no more than four persons each, scan through the Book of Psalms. Mark those psalms that look like they might be helpful to read during stressful situations. Discuss why certain psalms might be helpful in reducing stress.

BIBLE STUDY

Read Luke 10:25-28. <u>What do you see in this Scripture? How might your ability to manage stress be strengthened by appropriate love of God, self, and neighbor?</u>

WORSHIP

Invite group members to follow your instructions as you guide them through the meditation material offered in the main text.

Build a spontaneous meditation now. First, sit quietly and empty your mind. Breathe deeply. After a period of silence, speak words and sentences suggesting ways you may love yourselves—body, mind, and spirit. Trust each other and take your time. Let your spoken thoughts change into spoken prayers in a natural way. Trust this process. It will happen.

Pray for the concerns of your LifeSearch group members and for the concerns of the world. Jot down specific prayer requests to remember during the coming week:

Pray this prayer or one in your own words:

Thank you, God, for the wholeness of our lives lived through bodies, minds, and spirits. Help us inhabit them as we really are. Help us be ourselves, remembering that this is always enough. Help us believe, somehow, that this is true. Help our unbelief. In Jesus' name, Amen.

CHAPTER SIX

THE BEST WAY THROUGH STRESS

CHECKING IN

As you begin this session, be sure to take time for persons to share the events of their lives since the last time you met. Then discuss the questions in the main text.

Look back to the beginning of this LIFESEARCH experience. What stands out in your mind from your reading? What stands out from your experiences with your LIFESEARCH group? What one or two things have you tried as new ways to respond to and deal with the stress in your life? To what degree is the stress in your life greater or lesser than when you began this LIFESEARCH experience? Why has your stress increased or decreased?

She left work early to go and sign the divorce papers she did not want to sign. Later, she told it this way, "As I pulled out of the parking lot, I turned the car toward home instead of the lawyer's office. By the time I got to my back door, I was crying uncontrollably. I wondered what to do, because I was due at the lawyer's office. It came to me to get my Bible. I turned to the Twenty-Third Psalm and began to read it aloud. I kept reading it over and over, until finally the meaning of the words took over. After a while, I washed my face, left the house, and went and signed the papers. The power of God that day was the only power that was strong enough to deal with my pain."

An old woman told another story about the same Scripture. "I was being forced to give up my home. My children had taken my affairs out of my hands. I disagreed that the time had come. I cannot remember ever being so inwardly agitated. Strong and independent, enjoying life so much, it was more than I could bear. I know I was fretful and angry. I was so torn that I was not my former self, in a number of ways. What helped me most, on the worst day, was the Twenty-Third Psalm. I heard the words over and over and over. They seeped into my constricted heart, and I began to get easy. I still did not want to go through the next days, but God helped me, through that Scripture, to endure."

He said, "I looked up into the doctor's face as he told me I had cancer. I was not active in church. In fact, after attending early in my life, I had broken away and not returned. I cannot account for the fact that at that moment, after so many years, all I knew about God, deep inside, welled up in me and I faced the news without shock or despair. I would not have called myself a religious man. But at that moment, God seemed very near to me. Not only surrounded by my family, but also suddenly surrounded by God, I knew I was not alone and that whatever happened, I would be all right."

Another person witnessed to the power of God when she said, "When things get too bad, I get my notebook and write. I pour out all my thoughts to God. I tell God everything. Especially at night, pouring out my inner thoughts and feelings in that little notebook empties me, and I can lie down and go to sleep. I feel so close to God. My situation hasn't changed, but I can lie down and go to sleep. Things will be better in my life one day. For now, feeling God's nearness is the most helpful thing in getting me through."

Real Life Has Stress

<u>Real life has stress in it. It is a diverse event. The finest people have difficulties, tragedies, illnesses, hard relationships they do not understand, and tough situations.</u>

When all is said and done, nothing enables an individual to live through whatever comes, great pain or great joy, like a close relationship with God. Nothing enables us to keep life in perspective, weave life's events into whole cloth, and move forward in peace, like a close relationship with God. The cloth may have slubs—scars—where the threads were changed, but it is whole and may be even more beautiful because of the slubs.

God loves us personally, beyond all others who love us. By following Jesus, we may come to understand who God is and what a relationship with God can mean to us. Every person is of equal worth to God. Regardless of our station in life, gender or race, educational background, or economic power, regardless of marital status or the number and kinds of friends we have, we are all worthy. We are all loved and valued. Nothing can separate us from the love of God. Faith in God will enable us to live life with grace and power, no matter what our circumstances. No matter what, any person who chooses a personal relationship with God may live a life of usefulness and blessedness.

<u>Why is it so hard for us to accept the fullness of God's love?</u>

DISCUSSION POINT

To what extent do you agree with this statement?

What illustrations can you think of to prove or disprove the statement?

"The spiritual life is not a life before, after, or beyond our everyday existence. No, the spiritual life can only be real when it is lived in the midst of the pains and joys of the here and now."

(From Making All Things New, *by Henri J. M. Nouwen; Harper and Row, 1981, page 21.)*

DISCUSSION POINT

Stress and the Christian Way

In the midst of stress, whether the cause is inside or outside yourself, you cheat yourself if you do not listen carefully for Jesus' solution.

Countless human beings have lived beautiful lives, in and out of trouble, because they have believed this. Why not you? Why do you try making it some other way for as long as you can, before you give up, give in, and step into the arms of God? No one can truthfully tell you that pain and stress will go away and not come back. But many Christians can tell you that faith in God has worked for them in the worst times of their lives. Seek them out.

Why am I writing as though this is something you do not know? After all, many of you are already active Christians. Because all of us need to be reminded, over and over and over.

GROUP INTERACTION

In smaller groups of two or three persons, take turns sharing news of God's love with one another. Among the ways by which persons might do this include telling how they themselves have felt God's love, or helping someone else hear how God's love is being expressed to that other person.

When the pain and pressure of stress manifest themselves, as they do in every life, every person needs to hear again the news of God's love. Telling this news is one of the church's most sacred jobs.

You can say it better than I have. Do it now. Tell someone else the good news Jesus told. Regardless of whether you have ever tried telling it before, try telling it now. Pray for other members of your LIFESEARCH group as you do this. You never know when the latest version you hear will be the best you have ever heard.

A Focus on Knowing God

Let's focus on knowing God personally. No one knows what percentage of human beings ever do. But people do know if they have had a direct encounter with God. And "regular" people you know have.

Knowing God face to face is possible now. Knowing Jesus as a personal friend, brother, and savior is possible. Knowing the Holy Spirit as a real presence in the midst of a busy day is possible. From the beginning God has wanted a relationship with us.

Every person, made for love as we all are, longs for the right relationships in life. Every person longs to know and be known.

Other people, too, are essential for us to have the lives God envisions for us. God made us and gave us to each other in all the wonderful ways that loving relationships are worked out. Feeling loved, needed, and useful are central to life.

But no matter how long we put off a personal relationship with God, nothing and no one else can fill that place in our hearts and lives. Lives can be full and successful in terms of this world's values, but we miss the completion of really "having it all," if we never walk in the Spirit. Countless "successful" people at the end of their lives publicly grieved not having walked in the Spirit.

Make no mistake about it. Real life is never easy for long. The best resource for living it, stress and all, is a living, personal relationship with the One who made us all. People who have this relationship surround us and can help us find our way to it.

So how do we do it? How do we do such an outrageous thing as enter into a personal relationship with God?

Many ways exist. Just when someone tells you exactly how, God will enter a person's life in another way.

Wanting to know God personally is the beginning point.

Questions flood the mind: "What would it be like to know God personally? Is it really possible? How would I know if it happened? Would it be scary? Are people telling the truth when they say they really know Jesus personally, that they know God personally, that the Holy Spirit is really there with them? How can this be?

"If I were to come to know God was really there, how would it happen? Would I have to be in church? Would someone have to be there with me? Would I have to be alone? Would it scare me? If I got close to it, would I run, afraid of what God would ask of me then?"

Once, a gentle young boy with thick lenses in his glasses whispered, "I want to surrender my life to Christ, but the closer I get, the more I am afraid that he will ask me to do something big to show I really love him. Giving up my eyesight is the biggest thing I can think of.

"You see, my glasses are really strong. Because I have had a lot of trouble with my eyes and they are weak, my eyesight means more to me than it does to people who have not had this kind of trouble. If I give my life to Christ, will I have to give up my eyesight to prove I love him?"

Jon told me this at a church camp many years ago. I was hor-

DISCUSSION POINT

What questions might you add?

rified he had ever picked up such a thought. I have never forgotten the moment he told me.

Do those who put off opening themselves up to personal relationship with God fear what they might have to give up?

Julie went down the aisle of her church to make a full commitment to Christ. She said, "When I knelt, I was so surprised to feel not bound but free. When I stood up, after the prayers and benediction, I looked at my preacher and told him how I felt. He smiled the deepest smile and nodded his head. He said, "People always think they will feel bound, and as though they have given up everything, but they always feel free!"

Coming into a personal relationship with God so changes a person's life that even though he or she may subsequently suffer unavoidable, painful stress, a spiritual life will make it possible to persevere. All of us lose our way at times. We become overwhelmed by the moment's happenings and are swept away.

BIBLE STUDY

Read Matthew 27. When have you felt utterly forsaken?

We slip and fall into monstrous thoughts and feelings and act them out. Low self-esteem is epidemic among Christians as well as non-Christians. The best person I ever knew looked into my eyes in the last stages of her terminal illness and, momentarily exhausted, expressed doubt about God's love for her. Jesus also felt forsaken once (Matthew 27:46).

Knowing God does not mean you will never lose your peace and stability again. But outside the boundary of fret, anger, hostility, or tension, the One who loves us best waits as would any best friend. God waits until we cool down, come to, and look around. And when we do, God is there. The sooner we get started, the sooner we receive growing abilities to make healthy life responses. We learn to turn to God with our pain.

When we truly, at last, want to know God personally, God will meet us in the middle. God may even run down the road to us. Until then, God waits, lovingly.

DISCUSSION POINT

Read Luke 15:11-24, which is part of the parable of the loving father, also known as the parable of the prodigal son. <u>Does this passage help you to envision what has been described in the paragraphs above?</u>

Because we live in a world of plenty, in the fast lane or trying to get there, a relationship with God may not be on our calendars. We may choose to live without it. In reality, what we do is grow callouses on our hearts or let them turn to stone in order to cope with life as it is.

BIBLE STUDY

*Identify your feelings as
your read the passage.*

DISCUSSION POINT

*Take time to have group
members share the feelings
they identified as they read
the Bible passage.*

DISCUSSION POINT

*What do you think about the
friend's observation?*

Now read one of the most wonderful passages in the Old Testament: Ezekiel 11:14-20. Ezekiel received and gave the message that the Lord God would gather all those who had been scattered, remove the heart of stone from within them, and give them a heart of flesh.

Most people long to be gathered, given hearts of flesh, and live life unafraid. Many want to be able to be obedient to God, to love and be loved, and to live lives that count for something. What does it mean to you to live with a heart of flesh?

If you have a fresh desire to know God more deeply, talk to someone about it. Remember that many individuals have read the New Testament for themselves and have come to know God through the story of Jesus. Read one of the Gospels, each of which beautifully describes the life of Jesus.

A Few Last Words

I asked a friend to critique my manuscript before I sent it to the editor. When she had finished, she made helpful suggestions. I asked, "Looking back, is there anything that you wanted to get but did not get from any chapter?"

She said, "I think I expected to read, maybe at the end, something about trying to keep control instead of giving it up to God. With a knowing smile she said, "That struggle is stressful in itself."

For that, she got almost the last word!

WORSHIP

Take several moments as you end your LIFESEARCH study:

(1) Share prayer requests with each other.

(2) Discuss: Where am I in my attempts to manage stress? How does my spiritual journey empower me to reduce the effects of stress?

(3) Plan how and when you might come together again.

(4) Pray together.

Dear God, thank you for coming into our lives in a special way as we have talked about stress. Thank you for health, wisdom, and love. Thank you that you call us to receive hearts of flesh in a tense and driven world and to live in the world with these hearts, able to be your people, for ourselves, and for others. Forgive us when we bog down and fail to be the people you have given us to be. Thank you for the possibility of personal relationship with you, the greatest human privilege of all.

We love you.

In Jesus' name, Amen.

Afterword

One of my favorite passages in any book is the afterword in Henri Nouwen's *Genesee Diary* in which, after writing a whole book about learning to pray, he says he still cannot do it and keeps on forgetting what he knows.

When I was invited to write this, among the ricochet of thoughts and feelings was, *Why me?*

Three months previous to the invitation, I had been so stressed myself that I chose to make a silent retreat. I was filled with rage about something in my own life.

Writing this LIFESEARCH book while holding down a stressful full-time job has left me staring into the mirror more than a few times. I know my family and friends wondered if I knew that I was stressed myself.

I'm a chocoholic who gets on and off the wagon. I eat too much and go through periods of not exercising. I forget what I know. And yet—there is a trust, a sense of humor, a perspective, and a hope based on what I can remember. I will fall again, but the good news is it's OK to fall. Period. The good news of Jesus is that he called us to be perfect but loves us when we are not, just as he loved Mary Magdalene, Zacchaeus, and Judas. God sees the potential in us. God sent Jesus to draw us close and make us new.

So let's get on with daily life, wherever it is lived, with refreshed awareness that in a stressful world there is a way. By the grace of God, do it with joy!

THE LifeSearch GROUP EXPERIENCE

Every LifeSearch group will be different. Because your group is made up of unique individuals, your group's experience will also be unique. No other LifeSearch group will duplicate the dynamics, feelings, and adventures your group will encounter.

And yet as we planned LifeSearch, we had a certain vision in mind about what we hoped might happen as people came together to use a LifeSearch book for discussion and support around a common concern. Each LifeSearch book focuses on some life concern of adults within a Christian context over a six-session course. LifeSearch books have been designed to be easy to lead, to encourage group nurture, and to be biblically based and needs-oriented.

Each chapter in this LifeSearch book has been designed for use during a one and one-half hour group session. In each LifeSearch book, you will find
• times for group members to "check in" with each other concerning what has gone on in their lives during the past week and what they wish to share from the past week concerning the material covered in the group sessions;
• times for group members to "check in" about how they are doing as a group;
• substantial information/reflection/discussion segments, often utilizing methods such as case studies and simulation;
• Bible study segments;
• segments in which a specific skill or

process is introduced, tried out, and/or suggested for use during the week to come;
• segments that help group participants practice supporting one another with the concerns being explored.

LifeSearch was not planned with the usual one hour Sunday school class in mind. If you intend to use LifeSearch with a Sunday school class, you will need to adapt it to the length of time you have available. Either plan to take more than one week to discuss each chapter or be less ambitious with what you aim to accomplish in a session's time.

> A LifeSearch group is simply a group of persons who come together to struggle together from a Christian perspective with a common life concern.

LifeSearch was also not planned to be used in a therapy group, a sensitivity group, or an encounter group.

No one is expected to be an expert on the topic. No one is expected to offer psychological insights into what is going on. However, we do hope that LifeSearch group members will offer one another support and Christian love.

We will count LifeSearch as successful if you find your way to thought-provoking discussions centered around information, insights, and helps providing aid for living everyday life as Christians.

You might find it helpful to see what we envisioned a sample LifeSearch group might experience. Keep in mind, however, that your experience might be quite different. Leave room for your creativity and uniqueness. Remain receptive to God's Spirit.

You sit in the living room of a friend from church for the second session of your LIFESEARCH group. Besides you and your host, four other persons are present, sitting on the sofa and overstuffed chairs. You, your host, your group leader, and one other are church members, although not all of you make it to church that regularly. The remaining two persons are neighbors of the leader. You chat while a light refreshment and beverage are served by the host.

Your leader offers a brief prayer, and then asks each of you to share what has been going on in your lives during the past week since you last met. One member shares about a spouse who had outpatient surgery. Several mention how hectic the week was with the usual work- and family-related demands. Prayer concerns and requests are noted.

This session begins with a written reflection. The leader draws your attention to a brief question in the beginning of the chapter you were assigned to read for today. Group members are asked to think about the question and write a short response.

While the leader records responses on a small chalkboard brought for that purpose, members take turns sharing something from their written reflections. A brief discussion follows when one group member mentions something she had never noticed before.

Group members respond as the leader asks for any reports concerning trying out the new life skill learned in the previous session. Chuckles, words of encouragement, and suggestions for developing the new skill further pepper the reports.

The leader notes one of the statements made in the assigned chapter from the LIFESEARCH book and asks to what extent the statement is true to the experience of the group members. Not much discussion happens on this point, since everyone agrees the statement is true. But one of the members presses on to the next statement in the LIFESEARCH book, and all sorts of conversation erupts! All six group members have their hot buttons pushed.

Your leader calls the group to move on to Bible study time. You read over the text, and then participate in a dramatic reading in which everyone has a part. During the discussion that follows the reading, you share some insights that strike you for the first time because you identify with the person whose role you read.

You and the other group members take turns simulating a simple technique suggested in the book for dealing with a specific concern. Everyone coaches everyone else; and what could have been an anxiety-producing experience had you remained so self-conscious, quickly becomes both fun and helpful. You and one of the other group members agree to phone each other during the week to find out how you're doing with practicing this technique in real life.

It's a few minutes later than the agreed upon time to end, but no one seems to mind. You read together a prayer printed at the end of this week's chapter.

On the way out to your car, you ponder how quickly the evening has passed. You feel good about what you've learned and about deepening some new friendships. You look forward to the next time your LIFESEARCH group meets.

This has been only one model of how a LIFESEARCH group session might turn out. Yours will be different. But as you give it a chance, you will learn some things and you will deepen some friendships. That's what you started LIFE-SEARCH for anyway, isn't it?

STARTING A
LifeSearch GROUP

The key ingredient to starting a LifeSearch group is *interest*. People are more likely to get excited about those things in which they are interested. People are more likely to join a group to study and to work on those areas of their lives in which they are interested.

Interest often comes when there is some itch to be scratched in a person's life, some anxiety to be soothed, or some pain to be healed.

Are persons interested in the topic of a LifeSearch book? Or, perhaps more important to ask, do they have needs in their lives that can be addressed using a LifeSearch book?

If you already have an existing group that finds interesting one of the topics covered by the LifeSearch books, go for it! Just keep in mind that LifeSearch is intended more as a small-group resource than as a class study textbook.

If you want to start a new group around LifeSearch, you can begin in one of two ways:

- You can begin with a group of interested people and let them choose from among the topics LifeSearch offers; or

- You can begin with one of the LifeSearch topics and locate people who are interested in forming a group around that topic.

What is the right size for a LifeSearch group? Well, how many persons do you have who are interested?

Actually, LifeSearch is intended as a *small-group* resource. The best size is between four and eight persons. Under four persons will make it difficult to carry out some of the group interactions. Over eight and not everyone will have a good opportunity to participate. The larger the group means the less time each person has to share.

If you have more than eight persons interested in your LifeSearch group, why not start two groups?

Or if you have a group larger than eight that just does not want to split up, then be sure to divide into smaller groups of no more than eight for discussion times. LifeSearch needs the kind of interaction and discussion that only happen in small groups.

How do you find out who is interested in LifeSearch? One good way is for you to sit down with a sheet of paper and list the names of persons whom you think might be interested. Even better would be for you to get one or two other people to brainstorm names with you. Then start asking. Call them on the telephone. Or visit them

> **Interest often comes when there is some itch to be scratched in a person's life, some anxiety to be soothed, or some pain to be healed.**

in person. People respond more readily to personal invitations.

When you invite persons and they seem interested in LIFESEARCH, ask them if they will commit to attending all six sessions. Emergencies do arise, of course. However, the group's life is enhanced if all members participate in all sessions.

LIFESEARCH is as much a group experience as it is a time for personal learning.

As you plan to begin a LIFESEARCH group, you will need to answer these questions:

- **Who will lead the group?** Will you be the leader for all sessions? Do you plan to rotate leadership among the group members? Do you need to recruit an individual to serve as group leader?

- **Where will you meet?** You don't have to meet at a church. In fact, if you are wanting to involve a number of persons not related to your church, a neutral site might be more appropriate. Why not hold your meetings at a home? But if you do, make sure plans are made to hold distractions and interruptions to a minimum. Send the children elsewhere and put the answering machine on. Keep any refreshments simple.

- **How will you get the LIFESEARCH books to group members before the first session?** You want to encourage members to read the first chapter in advance of the first session. Do you need to have an initial gathering some days before the first discussion sessions in order to hand out books and take care of other housekeeping matters? Do you need to mail or otherwise transport the books to group members?

Most LIFESEARCH groups will last only long enough to work through the one LIFESEARCH book in which there is interest. Be open, however, to the possibility of either continuing your LIFESEARCH group as a support group around the life issue you studied, or as a group to study another topic in the LIFESEARCH series.

TIPS FOR LIVELY DISCUSSIONS

TIP 1

Don't lecture. You are responsible for leading a discussion, not for conveying information.

TIP 2

Ask open-ended questions. Ask: How would you describe the color of the sky? Don't ask: Is the sky blue?

TIP 3

Allow silence. Sometimes, some people need to think about something before they say anything. The WRITTEN REFLECTIONS encourage this kind of thought.

TIP 4

Recognize when the silence has gone on long enough. Some questions do fall flat. Some questions exhaust themselves. Some silence means that people really have nothing more to say. You'll come to recognize different types of silences with experience.

TIP 5

If Plan A doesn't work to stimulate lively discussion, move on to Plan B. Each chapter in this LifeSearch book contains more discussion starters and group interaction ideas than you can use in an hour and a half. If something doesn't work, move on and try something else.

TIP 6

Let the group lead you in leading discussion. Let the group set the agenda. If you lead the group in the direction you want to go, you might discover that no one is following you. You are leading to serve the group, not to serve yourself.

Ask follow-up questions. If some-one makes a statement or offers a response, ask: Why do you say that? Better yet, ask a different group member: What do you think of so-and-so's statement?

Do your own homework. Read the assigned chapter. Plan out possible directions for the group session to go based on the leader's helps in the text. Plan options in case your first plan doesn't work out. Know the chapter's material.

Know your group. Think about the peculiar interests and needs of the specific individuals within your group. Let your knowledge of the group shape the direction in which you lead the discussion.

Don't try to accomplish everything. Each chapter in this LifeSearch book offers more leader's helps in the form of DISCUSSION POINTS, GROUP INTERACTIONS, and other items than you can use in one session. So don't try to use them all! People become frustrated with group discussions that try to cover too much ground.

Don't let any one person dominate the discussion—including yourself. (See "Dealing with Group Problems," page 58.")

Encourage, but don't force, persons who hold back from participation. (See "Dealing with Group Problems," page 58.)

TAKING YOUR GROUP'S TEMPERATURE

How do you tell if your LIFESEARCH group is healthy? If it were one human being, you could take its temperature with a thermometer and discover whether body temperature seemed to be within a normal range. Taking the temperature of a group is more complex and less precise. But you can try some things to get a sense of how healthily your group is progressing.

✓ **Find out whether the group is measuring up to what the members expected of it.** During the CHECKING IN portion of the first session, you are asked to record what members say as they share why they came to this LIFESEARCH group. At a later time you can bring out that sheet and ask how well the LIFESEARCH experience measures up to satisfying why people came in the first place.

✓ **Ask how members perceive the group dynamics.** Say: On a scale from one as the lowest to ten as the highest, where would you rate the overall participation by members of this group? On the same scale where would you rate this LIFESEARCH group as meeting your needs? On the same scale where would you rate the "togetherness" of this LIFESEARCH group?

You can make up other appropriate questions to help you get a sense of the temperature of the group.

✓ **Ask group members to fill out an evaluation sheet on the LIFESEARCH experience.** Keep the evaluation form simple.

One of the simplest forms leaves plenty of blank space for responding to three requests: (1) Name the three things you would want to do more of. (2) Name the three things you would want to do less of. (3) Name the three things you would keep about the same.

✓ **Debrief a LIFESEARCH session with one of the other participants.** Arrange ahead of time for a group member to stay a few minutes after a meeting or to meet with you the next day. Ask for direct feedback about what seemed to work or not work, who seems to be participating well, who seems to be dealing with something particularly troubling, and so forth.

✓ **Give group members permission to say when they sense something is not working.** As the group leader, you do not hold responsibility for the life of the group. The group's life belongs to *all* the members of the group. Encourage group members to take responsibility for what takes place within the group session.

✓ **Expect and accept that, at times, discussion starters will fall flat, group interaction will seem stilted, group members will be grumpy**. All groups have bad days. Moreover all groups go through their own life cycles. Although six sessions may not be enough time for your LIFESEARCH group to gel completely, you may find that after two or three sessions, one session will come when nothing seems to go right. That is normal. In fact, studies show that only those groups that first show a little conflict ever begin to move into deeper levels of relationship.

✔ **Sit back and observe.** In the middle of a DISCUSSION POINT or GROUP INTER-ACTION, sit back and try to look at the group as a whole. Does it look healthy to you? Is one person dominating? Does someone else seem to be withdrawn? How would you describe what you observe going on within the group at that time?

✔ **Take the temperature of the group— really!** No, not with a thermometer. But try asking the group to take its own tempera-ture. Would it be normal? below normal? feverish? What adjective would you use to describe the group's temperature?

✔ **Keep a temperature record.** At least keep some notes from session to session on how you think the health of the group looks to you. Then after later sessions, you can look back on your notes from earlier sessions and see how your group has changed.

LIFESEARCH Group Temperature Record

Chapter 1
_____
_____
_____
_____

Chapter 4
_____
_____
_____
_____

Chapter 2
_____
_____
_____
_____

Chapter 5
_____
_____
_____
_____

Chapter 3
_____
_____
_____
_____

Chapter 6
_____
_____
_____
_____

DEALING WITH GROUP PROBLEMS

What do you do if your group just does not seem to be working out?

First, figure out what is going on. The ideas in "Taking Your Group's Temperature" (pages 56-57) will help you to do this. If you make the effort to observe and listen to your group, you should be able to anticipate and head off many potential problems.

Second, remember that the average LIFE-SEARCH group will only be together for six weeks—the average time needed to study one LIFESEARCH book. Most new groups will not have the chance to gel much in such a short period of time. Don't expect the kind of group development and nurture you might look for in a group that has lived and shared together for years.

Third, keep in mind that even though you are a leader, the main responsibility for how the group develops belongs to the group itself. You do the best you can to create a hospitable setting for your group's interactions. You do your homework to keep the discussion and interactions flowing. But ultimately, every member of the group individually and corporately bear responsibility for whatever happens within the life of the group.

However, if these specific problems do show up, try these suggestions:

✔ One Member Dominates the Group

• Help the group to identify this problem for itself by asking group members to state on a scale from one as the lowest to ten as the highest where they would rank overall participation within the group.

• Ask each member to respond briefly to a DISCUSSION POINT in a round robin fashion. It may be helpful to ask the member who dominates to respond toward the end of the round robin.

• Practice gate-keeping by saying, "We've heard from Joe; now what does someone else think?"

• If the problem becomes particularly troublesome, speak gently outside of a group session with the member who dominates.

✔ One Member Is Reluctant to Participate

• Ask each member to respond briefly to a DISCUSSION POINT in a round robin fashion.

• Practice gate-keeping for reluctant participants by saying, "Sam, what would you say about this?"

• Increase participation by dividing the larger group into smaller groups of two or three persons.

✔ The Group Chases Rabbits Instead of Staying With the Topic

• Judge whether the rabbit is really a legitimate or significant concern for the group to be discussing. By straying from your agenda, is the group setting an agenda more valid for their needs?

- Restate the original topic or question.

- Ask why the group seems to want to avoid a particular topic or question.

- If one individual keeps causing the group to stray inappropriately from the topic, speak with him or her outside of a session.

✔ Someone Drops Out of the Group

- A person might drop out of the group because his or her needs are not being met within the group. You will never know this unless you ask that person directly.

- Contact a person immediately following the first absence. Otherwise they are unlikely to return.

✔ The Group or Some of Its Members Remain on a Superficial Level of Discussion

- In a six-session study, you cannot necessarily expect enough trust to develop for a group to move deeper than a superficial level.

- Never press an individual member of a LIFESEARCH group to disclose anything more than they are comfortable doing so in the group.

- Encourage an atmosphere of confidentiality within the group. Whatever is said within the group, stays within the group.

✔ Someone Shares a Big, Dangerous, or Bizarre Problem

- LIFESEARCH groups are not therapy groups. You should not take on the responsibility of "fixing" someone else's problem.

- Encourage a member who shares a major problem to seek professional help.

- If necessary, remind the group about the need for confidentiality.

- If someone shares something that endangers either someone else or himself/herself, contact your pastor or a professional caregiver (psychologist, social worker, physician, attorney) for advice.

IF YOU'RE <u>NOT</u> LEADING THE GROUP

> **Be sure to read this article if you are *not* the person with specific responsibility for leading your LIFESEARCH group.**

If you want to get the most out of your LIFESEARCH group and this LIFESEARCH book, try the following suggestions.

✔ **Make a commitment to attend all the group sessions and participate fully.** An important part of the LIFESEARCH experience takes place within your group. If you miss a session, you miss out on the group life. Also, your group will miss what you would have added.

✔ **Read the assigned chapter in your LIFESEARCH book ahead of time.** If you are familiar with what the MAIN TEXT of the LIFESEARCH book says, you will be able to participate more fully in discussions and group interactions.

✔ **Try the activities suggested in BEFORE NEXT TIME.** Contributions you make to the group discussion based upon your experiences will enrich the whole group. Moreover, LIFESEARCH will only make a real difference in your life if you try out new skills and behaviors outside of the group sessions.

✔ **Keep confidences shared within the group.** Whatever anyone says within the group needs to stay within the group. Help make your group a safe place for persons to share their deeper thoughts, feelings, and needs.

✔ **Don't be a "problem" participant.** Certain behaviors will tend to cause difficulties within the life of any group. Read the article on "Dealing with Group Problems," on pages 58-59. Do any of these problem situations describe you? Take responsibility for your own group behavior, and change your behavior as necessary for the sake of the health of the whole group.

✔ **Take your turn as a group leader, if necessary.** Some LIFESEARCH groups will rotate group leadership among their members. If this is so for your LIFESEARCH group, accept your turn gladly. Read the other leadership articles in the back of this LIFESEARCH book. Relax, do your best, and have fun leading your group.

✔ **Realize that all group members exercise leadership within a group.** The health of your group's life belongs to all the group members, not just to the leader alone. What can you do to help your group become healthier and more helpful to its members? Be a "gatekeeper" for persons you notice are not talking much. Share a thought or a feeling if the discussion is slow to start. Back off from sharing your perspective if you sense you are dominating the discussion.

✔ **Take responsibility for yourself.** Share concerns, reflections, and opinions related to the topic at hand as appropriate. But keep in mind that the group does not exist to "fix" your problems. Neither can you "fix" anyone else's problems, though from time to time it may be appropriate to share insights on what someone else is facing based upon your own experience and wisdom. Instead of saying, "What you need to do is . . ." try saying, "When I have faced a similar situation, I have found it helpful to . . ."

✔ **Own your own statements.** Instead of saying, "Everyone knows such and so is true," try saying "I believe such and so is true, because . . . ." Or instead of saying "That will never work," try saying, "I find it hard to see how that will work. Can anyone help me see how it might work?" Instead of saying, "That's dumb!" try saying, "I have a hard time accepting that statement because . . . ."

OUR LifeSearch GROUP

Name	Address	Phone Number

FEEDBACK MAIL-IN SHEET

✂ CUT HERE

Please tell us what you liked and disliked about LIFESEARCH:

4. The two things I like best about this LIFESEARCH experience were

5. The two things I liked least about this LIFESEARCH experience were

6. The two things I would have done differently if I had designed this LIFESEARCH book are

7. Topics for which you should develop new LIFESEARCH books are

8. I want to be sure to say the following about LIFESEARCH.

9. I led _____ sessions of this LIFESEARCH book.

FOLD HERE

Thank you for taking the time to fill out and return this feedback questionnaire.

Please check the LIFESEARCH volume you are evaluating.

☐ Spiritual Gifts ☐ Health and Wholeness
☐ Juggling Demands ☐ Stress
☐ Parenting ☐ The Environment

Please tell us about your group:

1. Our group had an average attendance of _____ .

2. Our group was made up of
_____ young adults (19 through 25 years of age).
_____ adults mostly between 25 and 45 years of age.
_____ adults mostly between 45 and 60 years of age.
_____ adults 60 and over.
_____ a mixture of ages.

3. Our group (answer as many as apply)
_____ came together for the sole purpose of studying this LIFESEARCH book.
_____ has decided to study another LIFESEARCH book.
_____ is an ongoing Sunday school class.
_____ met at a time other than Sunday morning.
_____ had only one leader for this LIFESEARCH study.

Name_____

Address_____

_____

Telephone_____

Editor, LIFESEARCH series
Church School Publications
P. O. Box 801
Nashville, Tennessee 37202

STAPLE OR TAPE HERE